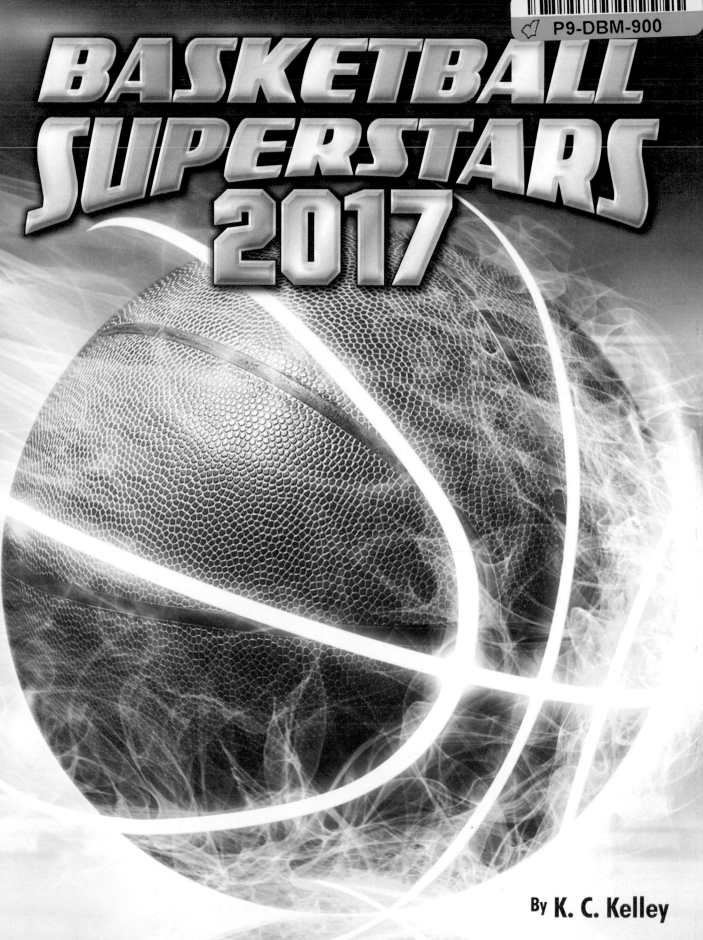

BASKETBALL SUPERSTARS 2017

By K. C. Kelley

Scholastic Inc.

Photos ©: cover: Igor Zhuravlov/iStockphoto; back cover: AlbertoChaqas/iStockphoto; basketball texture background throughout: Dewitt/Shutterstock, Inc.; basketball throughout: Billion Photos/Shutterstock, Inc.; 1: Igor Zhuravlov/iStockphoto; 5: Steve DiPaola/EPA/Newscom; 7 silo: Milos Kontic/Shutterstock, Inc.; 7 bottom: Kyle Terada/Pool/Getty Images; 9: Jonathan Daniel/Getty Images; 10: Jason Miller/Getty Images; 13: Stacy Revere/Getty Images; 15: Bill Kostroun/AP Images; 17: Eric Gay/AP Images; 19: Andy Lyons/Getty Images; 21: David J. Phillip/AP Images; 23: Ronald Martinez/Getty Images; 25: Ezra Shaw/Getty Images; 27: John Bazemore/AP Images; 29: Adam Bettcher/Getty Images; 30 top: Matt York/AP Images; 30 bottom: Chris Szagola/AP Images; 31 top: Julie Jacobson/AP Images; 31 bottom: Hector Gabino/El Nuevo Herald/TNS/Newscom.

ISBN 978-1-338-09865-5

10 9 8 7 6 5 4 3 2 1   17 18 19 20 21

Printed in the U.S.A.   40
First edition, January 2017

Book design by Cheung Tai

Due to the publication date, records, results, and statistics are current as of August 2016.

CONTENTS

NOTE: ALL STATISTICS ARE COMPLETE THROUGH THE 2015–16 NBA SEASON.

STEPHEN CURRY

Golden State Warriors

GUARD

■ **Height:** 6' 3" ■ **Weight:** 190 lbs
■ **College:** Davidson

Stephen Curry has shown that he can do it all on a basketball court. The two-time NBA Most Valuable Player ranks among the best shooters in the game's history and is a proven winner. But now he has a new challenge: how to rebound. No, not grabbing missed shots. Instead, he and his Golden State Warriors teammates need to rebound from a shocking disappointment. After setting an NBA record with 73 wins in the 2015–16 regular season, the Warriors lost in the NBA Finals to LeBron James and the Cleveland Cavaliers. As great as Curry's season was, it ended in sadness. Can he overcome the shock and get to the top again?

Curry started his basketball life on his home driveway, shooting hoops with his dad. Lots of players start that way, but Curry's dad was longtime NBA player Dell Curry. The two would shoot for hours at a time at home, but Stephen—his name is pronounced "STEFF-en," and often shortened to Steph—also got some shots in on NBA courts. When he was not in school, Steph would visit with Dell. Before the arenas filled up with fans, the duo would shoot around on the same courts where Steph would later be a star himself. For a while, the family lived in Canada, when Dell was with the Toronto Raptors. Steph even got to be in a Burger King commercial with Dell when he was a kid!

The family settled in North Carolina after Dell retired following the 2001–02 NBA season. In high school there, Steph was a star player. But there was a small problem. Though Dell was 6' 4" as a player, Steph took some time to catch up. In high school as a freshman, he was just 5' 4". But he loved to play no matter what. Even then, his skill as an outside shooter was clear. He made nearly half of his three-point

Super Stats!

- From 28 feet out to half-court, Curry made 51.6 percent of his shots in 2015–16. The rest of the NBA: 20.8 percent!

- From Dec. 1, 2015 through the end of the 2015–16 regular season, Curry made 308 three-point baskets. . . . That's more than the entire Milwaukee Bucks team made (306) in that span!

STEPHEN CURRY

shots! He grew, too, reaching more than 6 feet as a senior. He was still very skinny, though, and most major colleges didn't think he could play at the highest level.

Davidson College in North Carolina saw something in Curry, however. The school took a chance on him, and it paid off in a big way. (Plus, he grew to 6' 3"!) In the 2006–07 season, Curry was the Southern Conference Freshman of the Year and set a school freshman record for points. As a sophomore, he was the conference's top scorer and led Davidson all the way to the Elite Eight in the NCAA tournament. That was an amazing accomplishment for the small school—its best showing ever. In Curry's junior season, the team won the Southern Conference's regular-season title, but was upset in the postseason tournament. That same season, Curry became Davidson's all-time leading scorer. Next stop: the NBA!

Golden State chose Curry with the seventh overall pick of the 2009 NBA Draft. He was already a great shooter, but he also spent many hours in the gym working on other parts of his game. He knew he could not just shoot in the NBA. His hard work paid off in his second pro season. The NBA held a Skills Challenge during the 2011 All-Star Game Weekend in which players dribbled, passed, shot, and ran. Curry won!

In his third season, he had to overcome ankle injuries. He missed many games, and fans wondered if he was indeed strong enough to play with the big guys. But just as he worked hard to develop his shot and his game, he worked hard to get stronger. Connecting with special trainers and workout partners, he made a game plan to strengthen his legs and ankles. After several months, he was ready.

By the end of the 2012–13 season, Curry was one of the best players in the league. He set a new NBA record for three-point baskets—he would break it again and again! More important to Curry, the Warriors made the playoffs and were looking like a team on the rise.

The Warriors and Curry had an amazing 2014–15 season. He once again set an NBA mark for three-pointers, while adding a league steals title to his list of accomplishments. The Warriors won 21 of their first 23 games, and then stormed through the rest of the regular season and won their division. In the playoffs, Curry continued his hot shooting. He led Golden State to its first NBA title since 1975. The Warriors defeated the Cavaliers in the Finals. Curry was named the league's MVP!

TALKIN' HOOPS

TREY: The shorthand name for a three-point basket. It's pronounced like a dinner tray.

THREE Points!

- Steph's given first name is Wardell.
- He set an NCAA record with 162 three-point baskets in the 2007–08 season.
- Steph and fellow Warriors guard Klay Thompson are nicknamed the "Splash Brothers"!

In 2015–16, though it seemed impossible, Curry and the Warriors got even better! Golden State set an NBA record by winning its first 24 games of the season. The Warriors soon had their eyes on the single-season record of 72 wins, set by the 1995–96 Chicago Bulls. With a victory over the Memphis Grizzlies in the final game, they did it: 73 wins! Curry, meanwhile, put the three-point mark out of reach, hitting an incredible 402 treys (see box). Curry was the choice as the MVP of the league. In another NBA first, he got all the first-place votes for that important award. All that was left was another NBA title.

The Warriors almost got it. They struggled in some playoff games, but in the Western Conference Finals, they rallied after being down by three games to one to knock out the Oklahoma City Thunder in seven games. In the NBA Finals, Golden State had a three-games-to-one lead over the Cavaliers. But then LeBron James led Cleveland to some history of its own. The Cavaliers defeated the Warriors in seven games.

It was a tough end for the Warriors, but if anyone can put that behind him and move forward, it's Steph Curry!

RECORD RISE

HERE'S HOW STEPHEN CURRY HAS SET AND RESET THE NBA RECORD FOR THREES.

2012–13: **272**
2014–15: **286**
2015–16: **402**

LeBron James

Cleveland Cavaliers

FORWARD

■ **Height:** 6' 8" ■ **Weight:** 250 lbs
■ **College:** None

What do you give the NBA player who has everything? Something he could only make for himself. LeBron James had already made it clear he belonged on (or near) the Mount Rushmore of all-time NBA greats. He had a room full of trophies (see box on page 11) and NBA championship rings. But he didn't have one thing he really wanted: a trophy for his hometown team, the Cleveland Cavaliers. James was born and raised in nearby Akron, Ohio.

Why was the great James so focused on bringing an NBA title to Cleveland? Because he remembered how he started. The player who has everything spent most of his youth with next to nothing. James and his mother struggled to make ends meet. They had to move often and sometimes had to ask friends for a place to sleep. For a while, James even moved away from his mom to a family friend's house so he could have a stable place. Knowing what it means to struggle gave James a fierce will to succeed.

Tall and powerful as a youngster in Akron (40 miles from Cleveland), he found the place to succeed on the basketball court. In high school, he was one of the top players in Ohio and helped his team win three state titles. By his senior year, he was famous not just at home, but also around the nation. He won several player of the year awards. College was an option, but with the chance to secure his family's future—and with every NBA team wanting him—James made the rare choice to go right to the NBA.

James was thrilled when the Cavaliers chose him with the first overall pick in 2003. His mom and his friends could see him play often! And his big contract meant that he could always make sure his family had a place to live.

James proved he belonged right away, averaging 20.9 points per game at age 19 and winning the Rookie of the Year award. But he was just getting started. In 2006–07, he carried the Cavaliers to their first NBA Finals. The team lost to the San Antonio Spurs, so James was denied the chance to bring the trophy home. It would not be his last chance.

After the 2009–10 season (and his second NBA MVP award), James's contract was up with the Cavaliers. They wanted him back, but he wanted a title and he didn't think it could happen in Cleveland at that point. In a TV show watched by millions, he announced "The Decision" to join the Miami Heat.

In Miami, LeBron teamed with All-Stars Chris Bosh and Dwyane Wade. The team was built for one thing: a league championship.

Miami won the East in 2010–11, but lost in the Finals to Dirk Nowitzki and the Dallas Mavericks. That spurred James & Company to return, and in 2011–12, LeBron got the trophy he wanted . . . just not in the town he wanted. He was thrilled to win his first NBA championship, as the Heat beat the Oklahoma City Thunder in the Finals. James was the Finals MVP. Miami won again in 2012–13, and James repeated as the

LEBRON JAMES

top player in the championship round. He led the Heat to a fourth consecutive NBA Finals in 2013–14, but Miami could not overcome the Spurs that season.

With all the awards and the trophies and the praise for his amazing ability, James still wanted one thing more. To get it, he would have to leave Miami . . . and go home.

Before the 2014–15 season, James signed again with the team he had started with. The Cavaliers added talented guard Kyrie Irving and forward Kevin Love. That gave them the weapons they needed to power through the Eastern Conference. In the NBA Finals, Love and Irving were hurt, so it was up to James. He almost won the whole thing himself, but could not overcome star guard Stephen Curry and the Golden State Warriors.

Amazingly, James pushed the Cavaliers back to the conference title and the NBA Finals in 2015–16. Curry and Golden State were once again the opponent. The Warriors took a big lead in the series, and it looked like James's dream would end once again.

But then history happened. For the first time, a team came back from a three-games-to-one deficit in the NBA Finals to win it all. LeBron scored 41 points in both Games 5 and 6 as Cleveland tied the series. In Game 7, on Golden State's home court, LeBron had 27 points, 11 rebounds, and 11 assists—a triple-double! The Cavaliers shocked the basketball world by defeating the 73-win Warriors.

The parade in Cleveland said it all: "We love you, LeBron," the city shouted. LeBron loved them right back.

CROWDED CABINET

HERE'S A LIST OF SOME OF THE TROPHIES THAT LeBRON JAMES HAS TO MAKE ROOM FOR:

2004 NBA ROOKIE OF THE YEAR
2006 NBA ALL-STAR GAME MVP
2008 NBA ALL-STAR GAME MVP
2008 OLYMPIC GOLD MEDAL (US TEAM)
2009 NBA MVP
2010 NBA MVP
2012 NBA MVP
2012 NBA FINALS MVP
2012 OLYMPIC GOLD MEDAL (US TEAM)
2013 NBA MVP
2013 NBA FINALS MVP
2016 NBA FINALS MVP

TALKIN' HOOPS

DAGGER: LeBron has made a lot of these! A dagger is a basket that seals a victory for a team. It is the final big shot that puts a game out of reach.

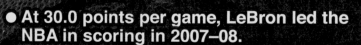

THREE Points!

- At 30.0 points per game, LeBron led the NBA in scoring in 2007–08.

- He's not just about scoring, though: He has been named to the NBA's All-Defensive First Team five times.

- In the 2016 NBA Finals, he was the first player to lead any playoff series in points, rebounds, assists, blocks, and steals.

ANTHONY DAVIS

New Orleans Pelicans

CENTER/FORWARD

■ **Height:** 6' 10" ■ **Weight:** 253 lbs
■ **College:** Kentucky

How fast did Anthony Davis grow in high school? His parents had to buy him a much longer bed! He shot up seven inches to turn from a ball-handling guard to a shot-blocking inside force. Davis has since become one of the NBA's top big men and has helped the New Orleans Pelicans greatly improve.

With big feet and thick glasses, Davis didn't look like he would be a basketball star. But growing up in Chicago, he suddenly shot up to 6' 10" while he was in high school. His height and amazing reach—plus a strong desire to be the best—made him a superstar. Every college wanted him, but he chose the University of Kentucky. He not only was the team's top scorer, but he also was dominant on defense. He set a school record with 186 blocked shots in 2011–12. The Wildcats roared into the Final Four that season and won the national championship. Davis was named the top player in the Final Four for the way he kept opponents from the basket.

The New Orleans Pelicans (who were called the Hornets at the time) selected Davis with the first pick of the 2012 NBA Draft. In his rookie season, Davis quickly showed that his defensive skills were ready for the big time. He was among the top shot blockers in the league.

In his second season, though, he added another big part of his game: scoring. In 2013–14, he led the Pelicans in scoring. He repeated that feat in the next two seasons, too, when he also ranked among the NBA's top 10 in points per game.

Most of Davis's points come inside. He works constantly to improve his footwork so he can battle the league's big men for the path to the hoop. In 2014–15, he led the league in two-point baskets. In 2015–16, he attempted more than 100 threes, too, showing that he is always trying to get better at the game he loves.

One tough area for Davis is injuries. He missed games in his first three seasons with ankle issues. In March 2016, his season ended with a knee injury. But if there is one thing his career has shown, he's always ready to grow into a new and better situation!

TALKIN' HOOPS

FLUSH: Davis's long arms give him great flush power. That's a slang term for a powerful dunk!

THREE Points!

- Anthony was named the nation's top prospect at the NBA Top 100 Camp in 2010.

- He won the 2012 Wooden and Naismith Awards as the top college player.

- He led the NBA in both 2013–14 and 2014–15 in blocked shots per game.

ANTHONY DAVIS

DeMar DeRozan

Toronto Raptors

GUARD

■ **Height:** 6' 7"   ■ **Weight:** 220 lbs
■ **College:** USC

DeMar DeRozan has come a long way to reach his spot among the NBA's best. The Toronto Raptors' guard grew up in a rough neighborhood in Compton, California. Two of his relatives were killed on the streets. Gangs controlled parts of his neighborhood. But his parents were determined that he would succeed. His father, Frank, often played one-on-one with his son for hours. Frank likes to tell the story of when 12-year-old DeMar, who was known around the neighborhood as "Deebo," dunked on him for the first time!

In high school, DeRozan was a superstar. He was a McDonald's All-America selection. Many schools wanted him to come play for them, but he chose the University of Southern California. A big reason was that it was a short drive from Compton, and his parents could see him play.

As a freshman at USC, DeRozan helped his team reach the championship game in the 2009 Pac-10 Conference tournament. After averaging 13 points a game during the regular season, he poured in 25 in the title game, and the Trojans were the champs. DeRozan was named the tournament MVP.

DeRozan knew that making the jump to the NBA would be a big one, but his mother was sick and he wanted to get his family a house out of the old neighborhood. He put himself into the draft and was taken No. 9 overall by the Raptors. By his second season, he was starting just about every game.

Even after he made it to the NBA and became an All-Star, DeRozan kept working hard. In the offseason, he plays in the Drew League in Los Angeles. He works out with trainer Chris Farr in Oakland. And he spends hours in the gym. That hard work has made DeRozan one of the league's toughest players. He has the power to bull to the hoop, but he also can step back with a sweet jumper.

All that was on display in 2015–16, DeRozan's seventh NBA season. He set a career high by averaging 23.5 points per game while also dishing out 4 assists per game. More importantly, he helped the Raptors win 56 games, their most ever. Then they pushed the Eastern Conference-champion Cleveland Cavaliers to six games in the conference finals. As hard as DeRozan has worked, he knows he has one more feat to accomplish: bringing an NBA title to Canada!

TALKIN' HOOPS

ANKLE-BREAKER:
A dribbling move that is so good, the opponent looks like he might break his ankles trying to keep up!

THREE Points!

- As a high school senior, DeMar averaged 29.2 points per game.
- He was named to the 2014 and 2016 NBA All-Star teams.
- He played for the gold medal-winning US team at the 2016 Olympics.

DEMAR DEROZAN

KEVIN DURANT

Golden State Warriors

FORWARD

Height: 6' 9"   **Weight:** 240 lbs
College: Texas

The only thing that has been able to stop Kevin Durant since he swooped into the NBA at age 19 was a broken bone in his foot. While with the Oklahoma City Thunder, the star forward had to miss most of the 2014–15 season recovering from surgery. So when he came back for 2015–16, the word to the rest of the NBA was . . . watch out!

Durant is the rare hoopster who combines height and reach with an accurate outside shot. He developed that skill as a youngster near Washington, DC. He loved the game, and he spent a lot of time on ball handling and shooting. Then, before his second high school season, he grew five inches! That also gave him the height to play among the big guys.

Durant chose to play college basketball at Texas and quickly showed that he would only be with the Longhorns for a short while. He averaged more than 25 points and 11 rebounds per game and earned several college player of the year awards. Next up: NBA stardom.

The Seattle SuperSonics selected him with the second overall pick of the 2007 NBA Draft. That was one year before the franchise moved to Oklahoma City. In Seattle, Durant was the Rookie of the Year. His all-around game made him an instant superstar. The Thunder made the playoffs in 2009–10, and each of the next four seasons, too. In 2011–12, they reached the NBA Finals.

Durant was always there — in fact, he led the league in minutes played three times . . . until the foot injury in 2014–15. That season, the Thunder missed the playoffs. He and the Thunder roared back in 2015–16, however. Durant averaged 28.2 points per game to rank third in the NBA. Oklahoma City won 55 games and made it to the Western Conference Finals before losing to the Warriors.

Then Durant signed with his playoff foes for the 2016–17 season. In Golden State, he'll join stars such as Steph Curry and Klay Thompson. So once again, the word to the rest of the NBA is . . . watch out!

TALKIN' HOOPS

POST UP: The post is the area beneath the basket. A player who "posts up" takes a position there with his back to the basket, ready to receive a pass and spin to the hoop.

THREE Points!

- Kevin was a high school All-American.
- In 2007, he won the John Wooden Award as the nation's top college player.
- He was the leading scorer for the US team that won the gold medal at the 2016 Olympic Games in Rio.

Kevin Durant

PAUL GEORGE

Indiana Pacers

FORWARD

- **Height:** 6' 9" ■ **Weight:** 220 lbs
- **College:** Fresno State

Talk about a comeback! Heading into the 2014–15 season, Paul George was one of the NBA's top players. The two-time All-Star led the Indiana Pacers to the Eastern Conference Finals the previous spring. Suddenly, all that success was in danger. While playing for Team USA in August 2014, George landed awkwardly after jumping. Somehow, his leg broke in a gruesome way. The great player was carried from the court on a stretcher, his future very much in doubt.

George was used to wondering what was next. He grew up in Palmdale, California, where he averaged 25 points per game as a high school senior, but got little attention from the major college programs. He moved on to Fresno State in central California. He starred two seasons for the Bulldogs before the Pacers chose him with the 10th overall pick of the 2010 NBA Draft. However, then he had to wait again. It was not until his second season that he became a regular starter. Showing the same sort of grit that helped him grow as a player in high school and college, George earned a key award after the 2012–13 season. He was named the NBA's Most Improved Player.

He had become an established star. The next season, he carried Indiana deep into the playoffs. Then he suffered his terrible injury. Some players would have healed and hung up their sneakers. Not George. He was determined to come back, no matter how hard it would be or how much work it would take. Somehow, he returned to the court in April of 2015, shocking doctors and his teammates. Then only a few games into his comeback, he strained the calf on his other leg. But coming back was nothing new, so he worked hard in the offseason and rebounded for 2015–16.

That year, he had his best season yet, averaging a career-high 23.1 points per game. He made the All-NBA third team as well as his third All-Star Game. The Pacers returned to the playoffs. They took on the super-strong Toronto Raptors and extended them to seven games before losing. So it's more comebacks to come for George and the Pacers in 2016–17 . . . then again, he's used to that!

TALKIN' HOOPS

BALLER: Nickname for a hard-working basketball player—a guy who gives it his all for his team every game.

THREE Points!

- Paul has a cool middle name: Cliftonantho.
- His older sister played college basketball at Pepperdine.
- He won a gold medal with the US team at the 2016 Olympics.

JAMES HARDEN

Houston Rockets
GUARD

▮ **Height:** 6' 5" ▮ **Weight:** 220 lbs
▮ **College:** Arizona State

There are lots of ways to score in the NBA. You can rain in a three-point shot. You can crash the line through the tall trees. You can float up for a mid-range jumper. You can stand calmly at the line for a free throw. And that's not even mentioning dunks. Only a few players can say they excel at all those ways of scoring, but one of them is certainly James "The Beard" Harden of the Houston Rockets. Over the past few seasons, he has become one of the NBA's most surefire scoring machines. And you thought he was just a guy with a cool beard!

Harden grew up near Los Angeles, where he led his high school team to a state championship . . . twice! He moved on to Arizona State and was a star there, too, earning Pac-10 Player of the Year honors. Next stop: the NBA.

The Oklahoma City Thunder took Harden with the third overall pick in 2009, but he ran into a roadblock for playing time. The Thunder had scoring machines Kevin Durant and Russell Westbrook, plus other veterans who started ahead of him. No problem: Harden worked so hard off the bench he was named the NBA's Sixth Man of the Year for 2011–12. The Thunder won the Western Conference that season, but lost to Miami in the Finals.

After that season, Harden was traded to the Rockets, who wanted him to be the star of their show. Harden was thrilled. He led the team in scoring his first two seasons in Houston. He led the entire NBA in total points each of the past two seasons.

The Rockets finished in first place in the NBA's Southwest Division in 2014–15. They fell off a bit in 2015–16 but made the playoffs again. Unfortunately, they ran into the buzz saw called the Warriors in the first round. Though Harden did his best, Houston lost in five games. Still, it marked the fourth season in a row that Houston reached the postseason. The big difference: "The Beard," of course.

TALKIN' HOOPS

THREE Points!

PULL-UP JUMPER:
A shot on which the player races to a spot, then suddenly leaps straight up to shoot. It is very hard to defend.

- James was an All-American in his sophomore year in college.
- He played for the US team that won a gold medal at the Olympic Games in 2012.
- He has led the NBA in free-throw attempts three times.

KYRIE IRVING

Cleveland Cavaliers

GUARD

▮ **Height:** 6' 3" ▮ **Weight:** 193 lbs
▮ **College:** Duke

Kyrie Irving always knew where he was going. When he was in the fourth grade, he wrote down his life goal: "Play in the NBA." He and his father, Drederick, spent the next decade or so working together to reach that goal, and in 2016, the Cleveland Cavaliers' guard and his dad were able to share in another dream come true: holding an NBA championship trophy.

Irving was born in Melbourne, Australia. Drederick, who was born in New York City and played at Boston College, was playing for a pro team in Australia as he tried to make his own NBA dreams come true. But when his wife died in 1996, Drederick returned to the United States to get a full-time job. After getting work at a finance company on Wall Street, Drederick moved his family to New Jersey, where Kyrie and his sister could be in better schools.

Drederick showed his son the skills and moves he had used. Kyrie worked hard and was an All-America selection in high school. He was a solid scorer, but also a great ball handler and defender.

Many colleges wanted Kyrie to play for them, but he chose Duke, a famous basketball school. Irving was eager to fulfill his NBA dream, so he left Duke after one season. The Cavaliers made him the first overall pick of the 2011 NBA Draft. After averaging 18.5 points and 5.4 assists, he was named the Rookie of the Year. The next season, he made the All-Star Game for the first of three consecutive years.

As great as Irving was, he needed help to take the Cavaliers to the next level. He got assistance in his fourth season when star forward LeBron James rejoined his hometown team. James's powerful game and Irving's ball-moving expertise combined to make Cleveland the top team in the Eastern Conference in 2014–15. Then, in 2015–16, the Cavaliers went all the way.

In the deciding Game 7 of the NBA Finals that year, Irving put on a great performance, scoring 26 points. None were more important than the three-pointer he buried with less than a minute left. It proved to be the game-winning basket, and the Cavaliers won their first NBA title. For the Irving family, it was a dream come true!

TALKIN' HOOPS

TWEENER: Most NBA positions are determined, in part, by size. But a guy whose size and skills put him between the range for two positions is called a tweener.

THREE Points!

- Kyrie is a citizen of both the United States and Australia.
- He was the 2014 NBA All-Star Game MVP.
- He helped the United States win the gold medal at the 2016 Olympic Games in Rio.

DAMIAN LILLARD

Portland Trail Blazers

GUARD

- ■ **Height:** 6' 3" ■ **Weight:** 195 lbs
- ■ **College:** Weber State

How quickly did the Portland Trail Blazers put the future of their team on the shoulders of 2012 first-round draft pick Damian Lillard? He led the NBA in minutes played as a rookie! But Portland chose wisely. Since Lillard entered the league, he has become one of the top young players in the NBA. He has improved his scoring average every season, reaching a career high of 25.1 points per game in 2015–16. That put him sixth in the league, up among players such as Stephen Curry, James Harden, and Kevin Durant. That's pretty good company!

If Portland fans had seen little Damian Lillard growing up in Oakland, California, they might not have thought he'd be their star someday. It was a tough place to grow up, with many dangers from gangs and violence. Fortunately, Lillard was obsessed with basketball and devoted his time to learning the game. By high school, he was a league-leading scorer and all-league selection.

Lillard went to college at Weber State in Utah. He worked his way up from Big Sky Conference Freshman of the Year, to conference MVP as a sophomore, to a spot on the All-America team as a junior.

The Trail Blazers chose him with the sixth overall pick of the 2012 NBA Draft and made him their starting point guard. He won the NBA Rookie of the Year award after averaging 19.0 points and 6.5 assists while playing every game. In his second season, Portland won 54 games and started a three-year streak of playoff appearances. In the 2013–14 postseason, Lillard drilled a 25-foot basket at the buzzer to clinch a series win over the Houston Rockets. It was Portland's first playoff series win in 14 seasons.

In 2015–16, the Trail Blazers lost some of Lillard's top-scoring teammates. Though that put more pressure on him, the team rallied and made it to the Western Conference semifinals before losing to Golden State. Lillard did get a running mate in fellow guard C. J. McCollum, who was the NBA's Most Improved Player. Together, they form one of the league's highest-scoring duos. With someone to share the load, Lillard is ready to take the next big step forward in Portland.

TALKIN' HOOPS

GYM RAT: An old-time nickname for a player who just loves the game and would spend all his time on the court if he could.

THREE Points!

- ● Damian performs as a rap artist under the name Dame D.O.L.L.A.
- ● He was the first player with more than 150 three-pointers in each of his first four NBA seasons.
- ● In 2015, he completed his degree from Weber State.

DAMIAN LILLARD

ISAIAH THOMAS

Boston Celtics

GUARD

■ **Height:** 5' 9" ■ **Weight:** 185 lbs
■ **College:** Washington

The Boston Celtics have won more NBA titles than any other franchise and have reached the playoffs 53 times in their 70 seasons. But they hit a speed bump in 2013–14, when they won only 25 games. They needed to shake things up, so they traded for nimble and energetic guard Isaiah Thomas. All he's done is lead them to the postseason in each of his two seasons in Boston!

Only 5' 9", Thomas has been battling the issue of his height since he was a kid. Basketball is a game that calls for tall players. Thomas will never be confused for one of the "bigs" on a hoops team.

Thomas grew up near Seattle, where he was a hoops lover from his earliest days. In high school, he was the player of the year in the state of Washington as a junior. For his senior year, he moved to the Kent School in Connecticut. He wanted time to improve his grades as he aimed for college hoops.

The move worked. The next year, he returned home to play for the University of Washington. Home cooking must have helped. During his college career, the Huskies won two Pac-10 championships, and Thomas twice was the Most Outstanding Player of the conference tournament. His teams went to the NCAA tournament three times. Even with all that, NBA teams looked at his height and wondered.

In 2011, the Sacramento Kings made Thomas the last player chosen in the NBA Draft. For his first three seasons, he was a very good player on a not-very-good team. The Kings traded him to the Phoenix Suns in July 2014, but then Boston came calling in February 2015, looking for a scoring spark. Thomas scored at least 20 points in 8 of his first 10 games in Boston and knew he had found a new home. Boston went on to finish with 40 victories, good enough to make the playoffs.

In 2015–16, his first full season in Boston, Thomas continued his high-scoring ways. He played every game and scored a career-high 22.2 points per game. He made his first NBA All-Star Game, and capped off his best season by leading Boston to the Eastern Conference playoffs. The Celtics lost in the first round to Atlanta, but that just gives Thomas a goal for 2017: to take things one step further . . . or more!

TALKIN' HOOPS

DISH: Not something you eat from . . . it's a nickname for a great assist. Thomas dishes better than almost any other NBA point guard.

THREE Points!

- Isaiah made a buzzer-beating shot in the 2011 Pac-10 tournament final to beat Arizona.

- He has more "win shares" (a measure of how a player helps his team win) than any other player his height in NBA history.

- His name is spelled slightly different than Hall of Fame guard Isiah Thomas.

ISAIAH THOMAS

KARL-ANTHONY TOWNS

Minnesota Timberwolves

CENTER

▌**Height:** 7' 0" ▌**Weight:** 244 lbs
▌**College:** Kentucky

Sometimes it can be hard to live up to what people expect. NBA fans figured Karl-Anthony Towns would be an immediate superstar. He could have struggled with that or felt the pressure. Instead, he came through. Though only 20 years old, the Minnesota Timberwolves' seven-footer was the NBA's top rookie in 2015–16.

Towns grew up in New Jersey. His height made him perfect for hoops. He was 6' 3" tall in fifth grade! And his dad was a coach who made him take 1,000 jump shots every day. But his parents made sure he was more than just a player. He learned to play piano, loved to bake cookies, tried golf, and even played Ultimate Frisbee. He was very smart, too. He graduated high school in three years with nearly a 4.0 grade-point average. When he wasn't hitting the books, Towns was helping his small private high school win basketball games. His school won the state championship in its division three times with Towns in the lineup.

Lots of colleges wanted Towns, but he chose Kentucky. He had met that school's coach, John Calipari, while playing for the Dominican Republic national team. Towns's mother is from that island country. Calipari was the coach!

Towns played only one season with Kentucky, but what a season it was! He was the best defensive player in the NCAA, according to the "defensive rating" statistic. In another stat called "win shares per 40 minutes," which measures how much a player helped his team to victory, he was also tops in college hoops. He led the Wildcats into the Final Four. As the NBA Draft approached, it was clear that he'd be among the top picks. Minnesota went first and chose him. The Timberwolves made the right choice.

Towns was a starter from his first game and quickly became a top big man. One online report claimed that Towns was doing everything better than every other rookie. That included outside shooting, inside defense, and even decision-making! He led NBA rookies at the end of the season in scoring average and rebounds per game. He also played every game for the Timberwolves. The team didn't make the playoffs, but with talent such as Towns and fellow high-scoring young player Andrew Wiggins, Minnesota looks to make some noise in the coming seasons.

TALKIN' HOOPS

THREE Points!

DENIED: Blocked, as in a shot. At seven feet tall, Towns blocks, or denies, a lot of shots.

● **Karl-Anthony was on the student council in high school.**

● **Thanks to his mother's heritage, he has played for the Dominican Republic national team.**

● **He wears size-20 sneakers!**

KARL-ANTHONY TOWNS

RISING STARS

Along with NBA Rookie of the Year Karl-Anthony Towns (page 28), here are the top first-year players from the 2015–16 season!

DEVIN BOOKER
Phoenix Suns
- **Height:** 6' 6" ■ **Weight:** 206 lbs ■ **Pos:** Guard
- **College:** Kentucky

The Suns know they have a winner in Booker. When injuries struck the club's starting guards, he stepped right up. He became an on-court leader and a top scorer. He posted 20 or more points in 16 games.

JAHLIL OKAFOR
Philadelphia 76ers
- **Height:** 6' 11" ■ **Weight:** 275 lbs ■ **Pos:** Center
- **College:** Duke

The former Duke star is in a tough spot with the struggling 76ers. But his powerful inside game and ability to handle the ball well make him a player to watch. He averaged 17.5 points per game in his rookie season.

KRISTAPS PORZINGIS

New York Knicks

■ **Height:** 7' 3" ■ **Weight:** 240 lbs

■ **Pos:** Forward/Center ■ **College:** None

The lanky player from Latvia became a folk hero in New York for his all-around play and positive attitude. He joined a Spanish pro team when he was 15, but always dreamed of the NBA. A big fan of American music, he joined the Knicks in 2015–16. They found a winner . . . and a member of the league's All-Rookie team.

JUSTISE WINSLOW

Miami Heat

■ **Height:** 6' 7" ■ **Weight:** 225 lbs ■ **Pos:** Forward

□ **College:** Duke

The Heat knew they had a scorer in Winslow, but they didn't know they had a Swiss army knife! After injuries to veterans, Winslow became the team's key man off the bench, filling roles in the paint, on the outside, and in covering tough opponents. Wherever he settles in once he starts, he'll be a star.

2015-16
NBA Final Standings

EASTERN CONFERENCE

Atlantic Division

Toronto Raptors	56–26
Boston Celtics	48–34
New York Knicks	32–50
Brooklyn Nets	21–61
Philadelphia 76ers	10–72

Central Division

Cleveland Cavaliers	57–25
Indiana Pacers	45–37
Detroit Pistons	44–38
Chicago Bulls	42–40
Milwaukee Bucks	33–49

Southeast Division

Miami Heat	48–34
Atlanta Hawks	48–34
Charlotte Hornets	48–34
Washington Wizards	41–41
Orlando Magic	35–47

WESTERN CONFERENCE

Northwest Division

Oklahoma City Thunder	55–27
Portland Trail Blazers	44–38
Utah Jazz	40–42
Denver Nuggets	33–49
Minnesota Timberwolves	29–53

Pacific Division

Golden State Warriors	73–9
Los Angeles Clippers	53–29
Sacramento Kings	33–49
Phoenix Suns	23–59
Los Angeles Lakers	17–65

Southwest Division

San Antonio Spurs	67–15
Dallas Mavericks	42–40
Memphis Grizzlies	42–40
Houston Rockets	41–41
New Orleans Pelicans	30–52